Volume Two

PUBLISHED BY GISS 'ON BOOKS
HALWINNICK COTTAGE
LINKINHORNE
CALLINGTON
CORNWALL
PL17 7NS

editor@scryfa.co.uk

EDITED AND DESIGNED BY SIMON PARKER
SUB-EDITOR: SHARON THOMAS

COVER: FALLEN IDOL BY DAVID PENPRASE

CHARLES CAUSLEY'S HAND BY COLIN HIGGS

© GISS 'ON BOOKS 2003
ISBN 0-9542150-4-4

PRINTED BY FOUR WAY PRINT SALTASH

OTHER GISS 'ON TITLES

A STAR ON THE MIZZEN BY SIMON PARKER (1996 AND 2000)
SEA HEAD LINES BY TONY SHIELS (1997)
PIONEER BY SIMON PARKER AND TONY SHIELS (1999)
THE SONG OF SOLOMON (2000)
CHASING TALES – THE LOST STORIES OF CHARLES LEE (2002)
'OTTER THAN A BITCH MACKEREL BY POL HODGE (2002)
DREAM ATLAS BY SCAVEL AN GOW (2002)
SCRYFA VOLUME ONE (2003)

Contents

Rag an Spyrys Lowena
For the Happiness Fairy

Subscribe and Submit

Scryfa is open to all and welcomes work from new and unpublished writers as well as established authors. Short stories and essays can be of any length to a maximum of 2,500 words. Poems must be exceptional.

Submissions and subscriptions are the life-blood of *Scryfa*. Subscribers will receive two copies of *Scryfa* each year, plus news, updates and invitations to events, for £10 (inc p&p). The deadline for submissions for Volume Three is March 2004. Send to: Simon Parker, *Scryfa*, Halwinnick Cottage, Linkinhorne, Callington, Cornwall PL17 7NS or email editor@scryfa.co.uk

Foreword

YOU wudden' believe what 'appened to me since the first edition of *Scryfa* come out. Well, truth is, I seen 'un. See, I was out walking up on Bodmin Moor one day when I seen 'un, I tell 'ee. Clear as day, right by Houseman's engine house. Ran right auver Cheesewring track, not twenny feet away. What 'a look like? Well, cat-like, definitely cat-like, you. Jet black. Black as tulgy 'twas. An' 'is coat was glimmin' like a slab 'o galena. Long thin tail trailing behind, like, an' 'a crept 'long like 'twas stalking 'is prey. Scared? What, me? Gyah. Though truth is 'a was gone 'fore I 'ad a chanst to sit 'an glaaze at 'un. Only got a lil' glimp really. Eh? What 'ee say? Naw, I ent told no police. An' I aren't goin' tell 'un nuther, 'fore you ask. 'Nough trouble as 'tis athout goin' knockin' for 'un, you knaw me. Naw, I never told no one 'til I saw you stanking up 'ome 'ere to Minions with that g'eat grin across your chacks like some chaney-cat. An' I looked at 'ee an' I thought to meself, I'll give that blimmer somethin' to chew on. What 'ee say? How big was 'a? Now let me see. Aw, must ha' been all of a foot an' a 'alf long. Lil' pink collar 'an a dinky bell, you. Gar! 'Ad 'ee there pard! 'Ad 'ee there!

Simon Parker
Scryfer Carn Marth
Linkinhorne Kernow
Winter 2003

Charles Causley

24 August 1917 – 4 November 2003

Ah, Charles, be reassured! For you
Make lasting friends with all you do,
And all you write; your truth and sense
We count on as a sure defence
Against the trendy and the mad,
The feeble and the downright bad.

– Philip Larkin

Below

Annamaria Murphy

for Mark Kaczmarek

A S Mary Robartes panted through the sweat, the memory of previous pain visited her limbs, her fingertips, the tiny hairs on her arms, the innermost chambers of her heart. She swore to the flaking ceiling that this one would not go below.

She prayed for a girl, but didn't expect to be heard as she was not a church-going woman. Sure enough it was another boy. The child shot out past the midwife and on to the kitchen floor. This was a good sign to Mary. It meant that the child was eager to get into the light, out from the darkness of her.

She named him "Lughes", which means lightning.

"That's how he came out, like lightning," said Mary. "He's dark like a storm cloud. The effort of him almost split me in two. Like a boulder, covered in black moss. Only a man could've designed a woman."

"That's true," said Jim.

And as she laughed, her milk came, and so did the tears. In later years the boy favoured salt on his supper.

Jim, her husband, could sing. His voice was as deep as Cook's Kitchen, where men sweated rivers 240 fathoms below. She first heard him sing in a concert up Trewirgie. She was doing the teas. His voice wrapped around her like a mist. When she served him his tea in the interval, she made the biscuit soggy from nervous spillage. His eyebrows, like black caterpillars, came just below the serving hatch. They married three concerts later. Lughes grew tall. His brothers had joined Jim down at Crofty.

"If you think Lughes is going below, you can think again."

"What else will he do?"

"He can work at the petrol station, go to college, open a shop, anything. Don't go filling his head with buccadhus, and ghosts and underground caverns. There's plenty to look at up here."

"Ah Mary, you don't mean it,
Soft in the night Mary,
Hard in the day Mary,
Mary who sheds no tears,
Mary who has no fears,
Mary whose eyes twinkle like Galena."

"I've got fears Jim Robartes."

"Mary who can read a man's thoughts
Through the fug of pipe smoke,
Through closed eyelids,
Under the sheets,

Only place she can't read them is down below. Fifty fathoms, a hundred fathoms. I've got me own thoughts there. Some I leave on the surface though, some words too explosive for a hundred fathoms. What else is the lad going to do Mary?"

Mary dreams of fast waters and tunnels, and men's voices. She wakes in a sweat most nights and can't remember why. She recalls that her father couldn't swim, nor her brothers.

"It's like you've been below," says Jim, "the heat of you."

Mary shivers, and Jim sings her a quiet song.

Lughes never went below, because Crofty closed, and flooded, and opened, and closed, and flooded again.

"Brimming over with tears," as Jim said.

Church-going or not, Mary thanked the Lord.

Lughes loved to surf, to catch the wave and shoot out from it.

For a while he had a job in a light-bulb factory, to pay

his way to Australia. He loved the delicate filaments that captured the light. He loved the way they flickered in a storm.

Views Of The Sea In All Its Squalor

Des Hannigan

All night we rode to windward in the face
of massive waves that heaved their grey-green
coils on to her side-decks, then raced unseen,
waist-high, and wasted to the sea's embrace.
The sea was in a rout; fear slackened all.
The night in havoc moaned beyond the lights.
Yet there was music playing far out and bright,
I heard its rise and fall.

One fateful lift, I thought, might cost us dear,
locked hull above and hell below;
locked widdershins amid the undertow
of tide and fish and blinding fear.
Those creature waves that rose like walls,
they struck and struck her groaning steel;
and thud, again they struck. She reeled,
but lifted through the frantic squalls.

In fighting mood he met the day,
his face bone-bleached and tightly braced.
Hardset against the sea's hard face,
he said: "We'll shoot, and make it pay."
Such times became my late sea litanies;
but I knew, in years to come he'd say:
"That was a breeze, mister, that was no sea.
I've seen real gales since then. You believe me..."

Helga's Gone Abroad
Stacey Guthrie

HELGA saw the words before she heard them. Like heat-seeking missiles they arced towards her, certain of their target."Stupid...Fat...Cow." Driving up Market Jew Street she had come head-to-head with a middle-aged boy racer who had decided that ownership of red, open-top sports car gave him the right of way at all times.Helga wound down her window and politely informed him that it was in fact her right of way. Well, when I say politely, Helga had her own version of polite. She had never fully grasped the strange human concept of not actually telling it exactly how it is.

Usually, when people had been "politely informed" by Helga they remained informed and went on their way with a glazed expression, like someone who'd been given a glimpse of the future and realised that no matter what they did they were going to become their mother. Not in this case. Mr Boy Racer responded with a sneer, turned to Helga and snarled those three little words. Helga felt like she'd been punched. As she drove home she tried to analyse the strange feeling she had and where it was coming from. What was it Mr Boy Racer had said that made her feel so bad?

Stupid? Well, that was patently untrue. She had a degree in Mental Health Detective Work (how to tell the clients from the psychiatrists) and an advanced GNVQ in Yurt making, using found objects. So she clearly wasn't stupid.

Cow? Well, Helga couldn't see the problem with that. Lying in a field all day, eating and sleeping – something to be commended surely?

That just left fat. Fat...ahhhhh that was it. Fat wasn't a word Helga was familiar with. It had never been required in her vocabulary. She'd always been more voluptuous than her Valkyrie sisters and she'd felt sorry for them. Now, as she looked at herself in the bedroom mirror, a strange metamorphosis was taking place. The curves she had always been so proud of were changing in front of her very eyes. She wasn't voluptuous at all. She was fat. Fat and ugly.

Helga threw herself on the bed and sobbed. How could she be so stupid? Why had no one told her? Well, there was only one thing for it – she would have to go on a diet.

The next day Helga went to the newsagents and bought every women's magazine she could find. She was very lucky as they all had diets in them that week. One advert caught her eye: "Lose 30lbs in 30 days with 'Why Weight?' We use foolproof, patented body-sculpting techniques to help you get the body you deserve. Your life begins here. Meetings in your area."

Tuesday night found a very excited Helga in the Little Jackie Memorial Hall. It was full of women of all shapes and sizes. A couple of weeks earlier she might have been chatting to them, finding out what they did, giving them hair and beauty tips. Now, as she looked around, she found herself thinking: "Ooh dear, look at Mrs Trevorrow's VPL (visible panty line). Oh, Sandra Curnow really shouldn't be wearing a thong at her age and, oh my, is that cellulite on Tammy Laity's thighs? The shame of it."

These thoughts were quelled by the appearance of a small, slim woman in spectacles, carrying a clipboard. A hush fell on the room as the woman cleared her throat,

"Ahem, my name is Maureen Sparrow and I would like to welcome you to 'Why Weight?' (*smile*). This is the first day of the rest of your life. You have made the best choice in coming to 'Why Weight?' (*smile*) where we have trained operatives using the latest cutting-edge weight-loss facilitation techniques. At 'Why Weight?' (*smile*) we have teams of scientists working around the clock to wrestle the deadly demon that is weight-gain, passing all their knowledge to you so that together we can make sure there is less of you."

Helga could not contain herself any longer. What were these techniques, this wisdom? She needed to know and she needed to know now. She shot her hand in the air. Maureen peered over her glasses and mentally calculated Helga's Body Mass Index.

"Yes dear – what is it?"

"P-p-please," stammered Helga. "Tell me what these wonderful techniques are so I can lose weight."

Maureen looked stony as she said: "You must eat less."

That was it! Why hadn't Helga thought of that – it was so simple. She would eat less, she would eat less than anyone. She could do it.

Helga threw herself into the diet. Luckily 'Why Weight?' (*smile*) had a huge range of products she could buy. They really were thoughtful.

The night of the weigh-in loomed large and Helga was as nervous as a kitten as she queued with the other women waiting to be weighed by Maureen. She stepped gingerly on to the scales not knowing what to expect. Suddenly Maureen was frantically honking a horn.

Helga jumped and wondered what she'd done. Maureen was beaming as she cried: "Oh, well done Ms Hormonal, we've lost 8lbs."

Helga was made "Loser Of The Week" and was so pleased at her certificate and sticker that she didn't notice the evil stares from "Golden Loser" Tammy Laity (who was secretly taking thyroid medication anyway). Helga was delighted with her achievement and couldn't wait to show Eric when she got home.

"Look Eric – I'm loser of the week," she cried

"That's wonderful darling," said Eric looking slightly bemused. "Are you ready?"

"Ready for what?" said Helga, pinning her certificate to the fridge.

"It's Bangers & Bingo night at Waterspouts – you usually love it."

"Oh no, Eric, I couldn't possibly," exclaimed Helga. "I've used up all my naughty points for the week and I haven't done my buttock clenches tonight – you go without me."

So he did.

Helga was in bed reading *Taste Or Waist – The Choice Is Yours* when Eric returned.

He slipped into bed next to her and cuddled up. He loved the touch of her soft skin.

"Hmm...let's make love," he murmured.

Helga sat up.

"Oh yes please!"

She brought out a calculator.

"I had an extra potato at dinner, so that's 20 calories. Let's see...10 minutes of moderate sex would burn off 15 calories, 17 for vigorous sex. So we'd better go for the vigorous if that's OK. And can we make it 12 minutes?"

Suddenly Eric didn't feel like it anymore.

"It's OK love, I've changed my mind. I'm just going to read for a while."

Helga watched in dismay as Eric rolled over. What was happening? They used to have a brilliant sex life. True, it could be somewhat unconventional, and she was glad the local WI had forgiven her for the slide show. It wasn't her fault they'd thought it was about cookery.

Surely the title, *101 Things You Didn't Know You Could Do With Chocolate*, had been clear enough? She'd never understand human women.

She wondered what was wrong with Eric – he was so moody lately. Maybe he was pregnant again? No, couldn't be, they hadn't made love in ages. Not since she'd started this diet. She felt put out – he could be more grateful. After all, she was doing it for him as much as herself.

The months went by and Helga kept on losing weight. She had overtaken Tammy Laity and was a "Platinum Loser". Maureen had even put her forward as a candidate for the 'Why Weight?' (*smile*) trained operative course. Things were good in Helga's life. Well, apart from her relationship with Eric, who was sleeping in the spare room. They hardly spoke anymore. Helga really couldn't understand it. She thought she knew Eric completely, yet she couldn't understand why he wouldn't support her success. She supposed he was jealous because men looked at her in a way they hadn't before.

Eric meanwhile was bewildered by Helga's obsessive behaviour.

"I can't remember the last time I saw her laugh," he complained to Jake Davey one night. "All she talks about is this bloody 'Why Weight' and 'Maureen says this and Maureen says that'. She knows the calorie, fat and carbohydrate content of everything – even paint! She gets blokes leering at her. They wouldn't have dared do that before, but now she goes all giggly and pats her hair. I just want my wife back."

It so happened that one day Helga was driving down Market Jew Street when who should come the other way but the middle-aged boy racer who believed his red open-top sports car gave him the right of way. Helga wound down her window and politely informed him that it was in fact her right of way. Instead of looking her up and down in the way she had become accustomed to, he turned to her and said: "Stupid...Skinny...Cow!"

Helga was gobsmacked.

Stupid? Well, we've been through that.

Cow? We've been through that as well, except Helga could no longer see how anyone could let themselves go like that – even domestic livestock should have some pride.

Skinny? That was an insult? It certainly sounded like it the way Mr Boy Racer said it.

Helga drove home and stood in front of the bedroom mirror. She was slim, there was no mistaking that. Maybe too slim? Helga watched as her reflection went through another metamorphosis. The slim, toned figure, she thought she had, was changing and suddenly Helga realised that she looked kind of...deflated.

"What have I been doing?" thought Helga.

She was thin – so what? She was still the same person. It just meant there was less of her. And that was a good thing?

Helga felt conned. Weight loss is a bit like a tampon advert, she thought. I've lost all this weight but I still can't ride a horse or roller-skate. I'm still the same me.

Or was she? Helga thought about Eric and how badly they were getting on. Poor Eric, he must have been so boring over the last few months. Helga felt as if a veil had been lifted from her eyes.

When Eric came home that night he found Helga waiting for him on the sofa, holding a bar of chocolate, two pints of Guinness and a box of chocolate éclairs. She smiled and patted the seat next to her.

"Come and help me finish these," she said. "And then we can go upstairs and burn some calories."

Mr Madaloni's Miracle

Jan Macfarlane

THE skies of Mr Madaloni's youth were broad, smiling, beneficent. The sun poured its bounty liberally. The earth was rich, generous, free with her favours. The God of Mr Madaloni's childhood was a Latin God in a Latin heaven.

For fifty years, though, Mr Madaloni had lived under a low, lowering Cornish sky, grudging with its gifts of light and warmth, rationing the golden days frugally, as rewards for fortitude in the face of cold grey drizzle and merciless winds. For fifty years Mr Madaloni had coaxed and cajoled the reluctant earth to bring forth exotic blooms, luxuriant foliage, and succulent, trophy-winning vegetables. The God of this land was a Methodist.

Fifty years earlier, in a time of turmoil and confusion, God had plucked him from his native land, attired him as a soldier, tried him and tested him through the ordeal of war. But then He had set him, like Adam, in a garden.

When the conflict ended the young prisoner of war was persuaded to stay among the formal flower beds and manicured lawns he had tended so well. Maria, the bride he had left behind after only a few short weeks, packed a battered suitcase and bade farewell to the little hilltop chapel, dear to so many pious generations of her forebears.

And so he had lived, the cycle of the seasons turning slowly around and around: fifty springs, fifty summers, fifty harvests, fifty Cornish winters. He was no longer at the big house of course. Retired, in his trim council bungalow, he kept the rituals of a lifetime, digging, planting, feeding, mulching, dead-heading – a constant, ceaseless procession, a worship of work. Maria was gone. She lay in the cold churchyard and no one spoke to him in the flowery cadences of his childhood.

His solace, his only consolation, was in work. In summer he would rise at daybreak and, barefoot, he would wander into the garden still clad in pyjamas to spray the groaning trusses of swelling plum tomatoes; imperfect, blemished, but plump and pungent like his grandfather used to grow. There were beans too, and sweet peppers – and all of God's good gifts growing there.

Mr Madaloni did not know when or why he had conceived the idea of growing – in the sweet open air, without benefit of glass or heating – an aubergine. He had nurtured the tiny seedling on the kitchen windowsill, sheltered the little plant in a homemade cloche, fed it, watered it, encouraged it, watched with pride as it burgeoned and grew. And now here it was – plump and glossy, inky purple, glistening in the warm September sun. A miracle.

This was his offering, his worship, his sacrament. A proof of the goodness of God made flesh. Firm, creamy, spongy vegetable flesh. He ran his cheek against the perfect unblemished taut skin of the aubergine, clean and smooth. He took his gleaming, specially-sharpened knife and deftly, with one sure sacrificial stroke, split the object of reverence in two.

His gardener's heart filled with pride and satisfaction at its perfect pale cream flesh. He sat for some time lost in reverie, contemplating the mystery of God, His manifest goodness, yet the sorrow of his Maria being taken from him. He felt the pain suddenly keen again and bowed his head under its blow. His eyes fell on his beautiful aubergine and he stared, perplexed, as its flesh began to darken. Faintly at first, then more distinctly, an image appeared, an image that he had gazed upon so often in the innocent days of his childhood in the little church on the hill. A sepia image in faded peeling plaster of the weeping Christ.

Mrs O'Brien from next door had not one moment of doubt. She fell to her knees in an ecstasy of praise. Father Peter, when summoned, was uneasy, troubled. Nothing in his theological studies had prepared him for this. Alarmingly, a trickle of pilgrims was already appearing outside the door. Father Christopher, older and wiser, urged caution. The simple faith of believers was to be admired but surely we lived in sophisticated times and the Church must not be exposed to the ridicule of super-stition. On no account should they say anything to the press. The bishop should be consulted.

But bishops are busy men. By the time he could free himself from his administrative duties the wondrous veg-etable was heading the way of all flesh. Corruption had darkened and shrunk it. A faint greenish bloom tinged its margins. It softened, liquefied, collapsed.

Mr Madaloni shrugged. It did not matter that they did not understand. The message was for him alone and he understood it perfectly. The God of his childhood, the passionate, demonstrative God, the God of extravagant gestures, the indulgent father whose anger is swift and terrible but whose forgiveness is like the sunshine after the storm, lived still. He lived still, and He was waiting for him.

On The Quay

Bernard Moore

As I was bendin' a hook one day
A furriner strawled along the quay.
His cheeks was white as gannet's wing,
An' he looked a whisht an' wakely thing.
His cloe's was nate an' spickety span,
But I sez to meself: "Now there's a man."
An' I sez to meself: "Now look at his legs,
They'm like a couple o' crabpot pegs."
An' I sez to meself: "A bit of a squall
Would blow his bones to the end of all."
An' I sez – but I didn' have time to say –
For a scraitch went up from the end of the quay.
Where a cheeld was awsingin' jest afore,
An' now there wasn' no cheeld no more.
Then a'most afore I could see him go,
That furriner sprang in the say below.
He couldn' swim much, but he keeped afloat
Jest while I tumbled into the boat.
An' I hooked him up an' lugged him aboard,
An' he had that cheeld clipped tight as a cord.
He trembled and shook, he was wake an' white,
But he awnly sez: "Is the kid all right?"
Sure 'nuff, an' he simmed to understand
When I gived him a hearty shake o' the hand.
I started abendin' the hook agen,
An' I sez: "There's different looks to men,
Braave hearts in whisht poor bodies bide,
An' looks don't count to what's inside."

Dead Man's Fingers
Carl Grose

THE *cosmos creaked, its mechanism stiff, its motor rusty. The planets had run aground, and the darkness was still. All had stopped. Nothing moved. The Maker of Everything frowned, for the Universe was buggered. Underwater something stirs.*

Archie: 'Ere Dick.
Dick: What Archie?
Archie: I bin sat 'ere so long, I grawn a barnacle on me ass.
Dick: If you 'adn't quit dancin' you'da bin barnacle-free, boy.
Archie: I given up dancin' cus you quit whistlin'. I can't dance if there's no toon to skip to.
Dick: I given up whistlin' when the Moon lost its will to roll round the Earth.
Archie: 'Twas a significant moment in the Grand Scheme o' Things.
Dick: And behold what 'as occurred – tedium 'as crawled beneath our carapaces Arch, and made our passion for dance go slack.

And with no moon there was no motion. And the oceans' tides yawned and slept. Stillness hushed the seas of the world. Fish wandered the vacant, useless currents without purpose. Whales sang flat in an empty, earless water. The Maker Of Everything fretted, and sent ripples of grief throughout The Infinite.

Archie: 'Ere Dick.
Dick: Yes Arch?

Archie: Last night I dreamt I was a Chinese Mitten Crab.
Dick: Say 'gin?

And the stagnancy became instilled. Picture, if you will, two crabs...

Dick: Brown ones. What fishermen call the "edible" kind.

...sitting in the muck and murk, at the bottom of Falmouth Harbour.

Archie: I 'ad a dream I was a Chinese Mitten Crab. And I liked it.
Dick: You what?! They Chinese Mitten Crabs, they dunno they're born! Swannin' about up the ruddy River Thames like they own the place!
Archie: But they're so refined.
Dick: Y'know, sometimes I question whether you was born a bleddy crustacean at all!
Archie: Meanin'?
Dick: Meanin' are you an aquatic arthropod or no, son?
Archie: 'Course I am!
Dick: Then name yer species!
Archie: Eh?
Dick: I asked what kinda crab you are, Pinchy.
Archie: Brown. A brown crab. What fishermen call the edible kind!
Dick: Then act like a pissin' brown crab, and be proud of it! Know who you are and celebrate the fact! Quit dreamin' o' being a toff-nawsed Chinese Mitten Crab 'cus I tellya this for nuthin': it ain't gonna 'appen!
Archie: Might.
Dick: Not in this lifetime, bud! It'd take a goddam miracle!

The sound of Heavenly Light, portending to something "miraculous".

Archie: Holy mackerel... Whas'at light...?
Dick: 'Tis emanatin' from across the harbour floor!
Archie: Dick! 'Tis Neptune offerin' 'is miraculous, transfigurin' power to turn me into a Chinese Mitten Crab!
Dick: Neptune be damned! If that "light" turns you into anything other than a bleddy laughin' stock you'n sling me in a clam-bake 'til me dead man's fingers steam!
Archie: I gotta see, Dick... I gotta knaw...
Dick: Where you off to, y'daft bugger?
Archie: T'ward the Light, Dick. T'ward the Light.
Dick: You never left this patch o' scud in yer life, Arch. You dunnaw wha's across that tundra!
Archie: (*nervous*) True. I aren't au fait wi' the geography what lies yonder... but I've a feelin' I'm about to find out! C'mon, Dick! Into the Great Unknown!

And with a frantic scuttle, Archie forges a path across the sea-bed, churning silt to clouds behind him.

Dick: 'Ere! Archie! Wait up!

They tunnel through the tangled forest of weed, spiral fast down outflow pipes, negotiate rotting wrecks, conquer sunken shopping carts and side-step the apocalyptic remains of the eastern arm of an incinerated dock. Until, finally...

Dick: Finally...
Archie: Aw my Gaw! That light! 'Tis more beautiful than I ever imagined... I'm goin' in, Dick! Goin' to Eeb'm! To meet me Maker! To look straight into the

Face of God! Neptune! Lord Of All Oceans!

Dick: I'll wait 'ere.

Archie: When next you see me, my friend, I may well be changed. Say goodbye to Archie the Brown Crab, and...

The sound of Archie bumping into a wall of glass.

Archie: 'Ello... There's a barrier 'twixt me and Neptune!

Dick taps it with his crusher.

Dick: Glass. Inches thick.

Archie: And there's movement beyond it! Colour! And shape! (*gasps*) Dick, look. That ain't Neptune...

Dick: Ha! Nuthin' but humans! Stoopid human beings!

Archie: They'm underwater. Trapped behind a wall o' glass! Poor buggers. They'm in 'Ell.

Dick: No, Arch. 'Ell is a pot o' boilin' water. This is summin' else altogether.

The two crabs peer through a window, a window into another world. Or rather, the Falmouth Maritime Museum. For the window is the viewing hatch designed for punters to peer out of. And as the punters peer out, the crabs peer in, bubbling with curiosity.

Archie: Poor, poor buggers. Look at 'em. Floatin' about like pieces o' drift. Shell-less. Pink. Soft. I pity 'em.

Dick: 'Tis the way of the world, Arch. The Moon is broken. The world's ground to a halt. The tide 'adn't the strength to push us back to our old selves. A life where once pride fuelled our hearts and made us whistle a toon for all the ocean to hear.

Archie: Has indifference chapped your lips so much you can't eb'm blow a note?

Dick: Has fatigue coiled like rope about your legs and toppled you from ever dancin' again?

Archie: Not for this brown crab.

Dick: (*proud*) Awww, thass more like it, Archie!

Archie: I see'd the light, Dick. And it's filled my bein' with pride. And when you're proud you wanna sing and dance. Tell the world! These creatures need a smile on their faces.

Dick: I bet they never seen a crab do *The Side-step Shuffle*.

Archie: It's bin a few years, Dick.

Dick: Gyah, 'tis like ridin' a bicycle, Arch. You never forget.

Archie: I can't ride a bicycle, Dick.

Dick: Neither can I. But let's take that risk, we insignificant things. I'll whistle. You dance

Archie: Oh, I'll dance. I'll dance 'til me claws drop off!

Dick: And together we'll make the world spin again!

Dick whistles a tune. Archie dances wildly, six little legs clicking and clacking away. And the proud crabs dance their dance before the viewing hatch. And the silt swirls, and the fish swim, and the tides pull, and the Moon begins to roll round the Earth. The Earth rolls round the Sun, and in this one significant moment, the Maker of Everything smiles a smile to fill the cosmos with light.

Weaving Winter Into Spring

Marjery Ruhrmund

Sunday School varnished childhood
when we sat on hard pine pews
listening to stories of a separate God
who looked down from pale distempered walls
and struggled for life in my mind.
Defended by my hardened heart
I spent years not listening
until it gradually dawned
that God was a metaphor,
a poor word to try to trap
the transcendent Mystery,
the Life in everything,
intangible and unseen
weaving winter into spring.

Lenny The Liar
Paul Farmer

IN the docks they called him Lenny the Liar. He made up stories, which he confused with the truth. But he meant no harm. He took early retirement and regretted it. He and Lily argued constantly. So he would roam the town wearing a yachting cap and calling people "Skip". Or he would sit with his friends in the shelter at the end of Prince of Wales Pier. It wasn't much of a life.

One summer's day Lenny noticed a young visitor couple at the entrance to the pier. He was tall, thin and bespectacled, wearing a broad-rimmed green hat. She was blonde and lovely. Both seemed bored. The man said: "Let's go on to St Ives. We can visit the Tate."

Lenny found himself stepping forward, touching his yachting cap and saying: "Tour of the town, Skip?"

"Lead on," said the man.

Lenny led on along Market Street.

"Market Street," he said.

"Why is it called that?" asked the woman.

"Really, darling!" said the man in the green hat. "Isn't that absolutely obvious?"

"No, Skip," said Lenny. "Market Street was built to provide work for disabled ex-mariners, who inlaid it with exotic woods from the mystical East. Its original name was Marquetry Street."

"Oh," said the man. The woman nodded to Lenny gratefully, and while her husband was looking elsewhere she kissed him.

Lenny liked that.

So he led them through the town and told them how the Great Fire of London had started in Falmouth; how dinosaurs had roamed Kimberley Park until the 1930s; how the Thirty Years War had spent its teenage years on Bar Road. When he finished they gave him twenty pounds. And the morning was still only half gone.

At home, he made himself a couple of boards advertising *Lenny's Lecture Tours*, then set them up on the pier. At the appointed time, a crowd was waiting.

The following weeks were fine. Lenny made money and, even better, he felt useful. His version of Falmouth and the real thing had little in common, but the tourists were happy.

Edwina Foulds, the noted local historian, was a celebrity through her regular features on Radio Cornwall, *Downalong Old Falmouth Town, Where Us Do Live To*. She came from Croydon. As Lenny's tours became popular, Edwina's own *Whileaway Tours* suffered. One afternoon nobody came at all.

"That's it!" she said to herself.

The next day Edwina joined Lenny's large party. She choked back her scorn as Lenny claimed that Falmouth's chief export is dung. She suffered in silence as he insisted that the Visigoths used to come to Falmouth on their holidays. But when, as they stood upon the steep bank of the Plague cemetery, he told them the modern lavatory was invented in Flushing and that the Mayor of Falmouth also has jurisdiction over Berlin, she could contain herself no longer.

"Liar!" she cried, and assailed Lenny with her full knowledge of Falmouth. Henry the Eighth she hurled at his head; she condemned him with Cavaliers; she seized him by the Arwenacks. She told of the Packet ships and the news of the death of Nelson. She gave a minute-by-minute history of the docks and closed by foretelling the second coming of Peter de Savary.

The crowd had grown, local and visitor side by side,

silent there above the town. Lenny stood, eyes cast down, exposed at last.

Then he raised his head, adjusted his yachting cap and spoke.

"Falmouth," he said, "was created in the year 1894 as a secret love nest for Prince Bertie of Wales' bits of stuff. When they threatened to expose Bertie in the tabloid press, Falmouth was reinvented as an ancient seaport town. All the people who live here, and everywhere else in Cornwall, are actors wearing costumes and only pretending to talk funny. And the like of her," – he indicated Edwina Foulds – "are paid lots of money to make visitors think it's all real. Now, you can believe her or you can believe me. 'Tis up to you."

The crowd stood, thousands strong, in stunned silence. Lenny turned away.

"Now," he said. "We will walk to Cliff Road, named after the pop singer Cliff Richard on the occasion of his knighthood."

And, with only the briefest hesitation, the crowd moved off behind him.

Lovesong

Dennis Gould

for Miriam and Kenneth Patchen

Say the word love
And we shall see
How the groundown
Long to be free.

Say the word love,
Look me in the eyes,
Open your arms, love,
See liberty among the lies.

Say the word love,
Reveal your breasts,
Open your thighs, love,
Show me your nakedness.

Obey no laws, love,
Government is nothing free.
Say the word love,
Move in with me.

When The Wind Changes

Stephen Hall

THERE was a twisted tree grew right through the roof of the house. Across the road. Just across from my bedroom window. It was the tree I grew up with and the tree grew up with me – nudging through the slate. Day by day. Year by year.

I never knew its name. But then it never knew mine. We got along well enough in our different ways. Being neighbours. I never saw its roots under the big roof.

My father knew all about the tree. 'Cause I asked. He told me how it was. A boy swallowed an apple pip, all accidentally, and a little tree grew inside him 'til he swelled up awful and died. So his Mum and Dad buried him in a slatey house. And that was the end of that. But it wasn't. Because all the time he was earthy dead the tree was alive feeding on the skin and bones. One surprising spring the tree grew right out of his tummy and out of the ground. It went right on going. Straight up through the roof. And that's how he was remembered by everyone in the village. So they never cut it down, see. Dad always sliced his apples with a knife and laid the deadly pips around the plate rim. I do the same. Don't you?

When the big winds blew on inky nights I could hear splinters of slate skittering and slipping down into the launders. My friend, the tree, lurched and trembled in its house. After – down on the road when the wind blew through – black slate flakes lay like old snow. When the Ragman came Thursdays the iron wheels of his cart ground the flakes to flour. If it stayed dry the workhouse people passed by in hopeless parties of old men and women – all separated up. Their hobnails pestled the black flour into dust. Then along came the rain and whisked the rocky crusty dust into cream. And off it washed down Madron Hill – as far as Heamoor, sometimes. When my brother came off his bike and knocked out his front teeth I considered it was mostly due to the slushy slate dust on the hill. This incident brought the tree and I quite close together. We had a shared hatred of my brother.

Mr Bennetts lived in the house next to the tree. Every week he'd drop in a copy of *Farmer's Weekly* for me. Mother said Mr Bennetts was very kind. And Mother was always insistent I went across the road to thank Mr Bennetts. "Thank you for the *Farmer's Weekly*, Mr Bennetts," I would say. "That's all right my son," he would say, patting me on the head in that way that very old people do. This went on every week for years and years. 'Til I was nearly eight and a half. Then the weekly presentation stopped short and Father took to wearing a black tie. Days later I found out that the two occurrences were connected. On one night when the big winds came a tree slapped down right on top of Mr Bennetts' Austin after a Whist Drive. Squished him as flat as a beetle. I never knew Mr Bennetts really – but I was very glad he was dead. As far as comics go, *Farmers Weekly* did not rate. The pictures were mostly the same. I soon tired of tracing Massey Fergusons, ploughs and grey forlorn sheep looking vacantly out of the pages.

Most of the animals were fat. So were the farmers. They smiled in gumboots, wearing grey doctors' coats. The fat, doomed animals wore ridiculous rosettes. I might have wanted to be a farmer had it not been for the kind Mr Bennetts. I put it all down to the tree knowing about the *Farmer's Weekly*. This increased our friendship significantly.

When the big winds blew, other things could happen too. A big wind can jump down into your throat and suck your breathing out. It doesn't matter if you crawl on the ground or walk backwards – because the wind is twisty. It's always looking for a place to get in. When the big winds blew, things could change.

I never played with the Skinners. They were on the new estate. Mother said they were a "bad influence". I never actually saw a Skinner but I always ran away at the prospect of seeing them. I knew they would strip the skin off nice boys like me and hang it in the tree through the roof 'til it all dried up like dead summer leaves.

When the wind blew it could do other things too. I saw what it did to Mr Roberts. Mr Roberts sat on the seat near the shop. He was there when I got on the bus for school and he was there when I got off. I think he was there all the time. He was all twisted up with a topsy-turvy face. He dribbled. Couldn't say two words together. Mother said it was because he didn't fight in the war. And he was a coward. God punished him, she said.

He was "afflicted" because he was "wicked". He must have been a very bad man. Mr Roberts lived with his mother and never got married. That proved it.

We used to pull faces at him. He'd get so aeriated it would make us laugh. My Dad got to hear. One day he said: "Don't make faces 'cause one day the wind will change and you'll stay like that." I thought about Mr Roberts. I never did it again.

The tree in the roof is still there. I wonder if another small boy has battled with the bafflement of it all.

Flakes of black slate will be on the road tonight. The Ragman is gone. The workhouse at *Tallyho* is long forgotten. After the wind, the rain will whisk the rocky crusty slatey dust to cream and wash it off down Madron Hill. Even as far as Heamoor...sometimes.

Marner Y Worhel Terrys
A Shipwrecked Sailor

Mick Paynter

Aswa yn fos a vor troblys
An dowr diswrys war vordonnow plos.
Yth esa ow tos den skwith pur demprys.
Skwith ha temprys y teuth an den,
Dhe'n porth a ven, porth byghan mar glys,
Y blesour sawrys dh'y bowes hepken.

A gap in a wall of a troubled sea,
The water broken on dirty waves.
There was a tired man coming, very subdued.
Tired and tamed the man came
To the stone harbour, a little haven so cosy,
Its pleasure tasted only in his resting.

Tom Bowcock's Eve
1981

Martin Green

I think of Richard Murphy's boat
The Galway hooker that could float
And cork-like take the wildest sea
(No waves before so frightened me)
As we came back from Boffin's isles
Riding the seas that seemed ten miles
From landfall and the Cleggan Quay,
The Pier Hotel, security.
How Murphy took a local tale
And hung a poem from that nail,
It told of fisherman Cleggan lost
Swallowed up in the mad storm's host
And of the seas that spelt disaster
When tides came up to overmaster
A hooker such as his, the lives
Of all who sailed; and of the wives
Who widows were by break of day
After the night was prayed away.
And then I think of that gentlest
Of men, a Jesuit, but best
A humble poet who, like Blake,
Saw beauty in the heart's own quake
And how he used his pen to tell
The tolling of the Deutschland's bell
When that ship shackled by the sea
Broke up to meet her destiny
Pre-figured in the unseen stars,
Enacted in her broken spars.

And next I think of Kipling's lay
Whose lines can sweep the breath away,
The harp song of bereft Dane women
Whose grief was in the very semen
Their husbands carried to the sea
Which took their lives tumultuously.
And now I sit a mile or two
From where the Mousehole lifeboat crew
Took off a week ago today
From the safe shelter of Mount's Bay,
Eight ordinary men you might
Sit down with on a pleasant night,
Plucked from their common joys by fate
To leave their homes, the glowing grate,
And pit their strength against the sea
Ruinously running free.
On such a night as this we know
Skill, strength and luck are simply no
Answer to the darkest waters
Which tears good fathers from their daughters.
The lifeboat found the crippled ship
She having let all caution rip
And had off-taken three or four,
Was pausing to retrieve some more
When the new coaster turned about
And dashed the lifeboat's engines out.
No black box, log or living soul
Survives to tell us of the deep hole
That swallowed up the cox and crew,
An untried boat, a master new,
And smashed the maiden voyaging ship
Venturing on her ill-starred trip,
To end upon the rocky shore.
Whatever cost there yet was more,
Those sixteen lives and sixteen hearts

Would leave behind their broken parts;
So shall I list the names of these
Whose lives were snuffed out by the seas?
The cox-cum-skipper and the crew
Who drowned with hope they might win through?
Or the roster of those men
Wrenched so abruptly from our ken
Whose bodies were thrown on the shore
Like so much rain against the door?
Their names belong upon a stone
Beneath which should lie honoured bone.
But for the most there wasn't much,
A limb, some entrails, just a touch;
Their death came swiftly in the night
And left their hearts not time to fright;
Here lies a foot and here a hand
And here some innards rope the sand;
Oh, here's an eyeball rolled in tar
And here an arm with no guide-star;
Stand the old saying on its head
It is the quick bury the dead.
Now safe in recollection's balm
And reassured by land-locked calm
I write upon a whitened page
The toll the sea took in its rage.
There's nothing, nothing, nothing can
Bring back the snatched life of a man
When he goes down into the deep
To sleep the last and final sleep;
Nor widow's tears nor children's grief
Bring back what's stolen by that thief.
December has deceitful seas
That bring to fishermen unease
Nor would a wise man take a boat
Upon the water's treacherous coat

And seek to leave the shore from whence
He was forewarned by common sense.
Tom Bowcock's Eve came round this year,
No songs were sung, no cups of cheer
Lifted to toast the good man's soul
Who was the saviour of Mousehole.
No fishes' tails looked at the sky
From Bowcock's starry-gazey pie;
No lovely place, you may believe,
Was Mousehole on this Bowcock's Eve,
And no one there would want to wish
On seven sorts of sea-borne fish.
The catch that night found by the waves
Was salted in the water's graves;
And Pol de Leon's church on high
Looked out over spume-laden sky.
How dare we talk when wind-filled lungs
Know not of those who slipped the wrungs
And sank and bobbed upon the sea,
Whose legs were broken at the knee?
Full fathom-five the husband lies
And lobsters feed upon his eyes
So never, ever choose to cross
The bourn that ever leaves a loss.
Fish die on land and men at sea,
The elements rule separately,
There is no market for ill-sense
And when for pounds, shillings or pence
We weigh men on the scales of life
There's not a child, nor yet a wife
Would put a heap of silver coin
Against the comfort of her loin
That engenders the growing seed
Fulfiling life's most urgent need.
Down in his locker Davy Jones

Plays dice with men's salt-whitened bones;
The sea rakes shingles on the beach
While polishing the bones of each;
Intrepid men who nets have shot
Lie close beside a lobster pot
And when you eat your new-bought crab
Know as you must a painful stab;
It took the changing flesh of those
Whose fingers rattle with their toes.
The sea throws up its precious fruit
A fisher's foot caught in a boot;
For every pearl the oyster rolls
Some living men give up their souls,
The scavengers that scour the rocks
Pick up and spurn the dead men's socks,
The lobster on the polished plate
Has picked some human meat of late;
The crab that's pasted in the pot
Once picked a man who now is not.
What consolation can we take
When men like these were born to break?
Save only that these men have died
While many others would not have tried
To stand outside themselves to save
Those threatened mortals from the grave;
For some men pass their lives asleep
And find the mysterious too deep
Embedded in the bowels of Christ.
For most men's courage is not priced
And once the rocks threaten the boat
They'll die to keep the thing afloat.
The widows, children, who survived,
Know to their bone their men contrived
To save imperilled people when
Their chances were not one in ten.

Most mortal men go to the grave
Unasked another's life to save.
Though nothing will bring good men back
And mourning is an awful black,
Spring follows winter and the snow
Will make way for the seed to grow.
Death wipes the slate and leaves it dark
That other names might scratch a mark;
For all our names are water-writ,
John Keats, his very soul out-spit,
And Shelley's corpse burnt on the sand
Agnostic heart plucked out by hand
From the ephemeral fire of doubt
Which by an act of God went out.
The rage is spent, and gently struck
The quay night-bell rings over ruck,
The wrack and wreckage of the storm;
South-westerlies now blow in warm,
However deep you look or down
You won't find Solomon Browne:
Her pieces lie upon the shore,
A plank, a hinge that held a door
Gleams brightly in the tarry wreck;
A scavenger fills up his sack,
Down, down, down went Solomon Browne,
Did fate ordain her crew would drown?
Hindsight is the most bitter when
We count the cost in lives of men;
Ask Lloyds if they insure tars
Against what's written in the stars,
Or whose the hand that holds the pen
That wrote the sentence on these men?
From sea we come, to sea return,
No ashes lie in water's urn,
As clay returns again to dust

So sea dissolves the flesh and must
When once the lungs release the crown
Render all life-born matter down
To the fluid, primal state
Where life itself was generate;
All falls, all falls, and wind and waves
And silence settles on the graves.

The Penlee Lifeboat, Solomon Browne, was lost with all hands on 19th December 1981 in atrocious sea conditions. With winds at hurricane force 12 gusting to 90 knots, the eight lifeboatmen put to sea in an attempt to rescue those on board the coaster Union Star, which had foundered between Tater-du Lighthouse and Boscowan Point. The pilot of a naval helicopter said of the lifeboat crew (William Trevelyan Richards, James Stephen Madron, Nigel Brockman, John Robert Blewett, Charles Thomas Greenhaugh, Kevin Smith, Barrie Robertson Torrie, Gary Lee Wallis): "They were truly the greatest eight men I have ever seen."

Sliding Rock

Bert Biscoe

We wore the ass out of hundreds of trousers
and left the tails of a thousand squeals
hanging like bunting on the Easter gales –

we slid like silver waters; like pitching boats
down the backs of grey-green swells,
and we panted for the fun of it like blowing whales.

And always in the scramble back up the rock,
looking up to the castle – dark, moody walls
with witchy-eyed windows – laughing at crow-calls

screeching low across tough meaty old clouds
which spread their penetrating drizzle and mist
like love right through to the threads of our vest

and we slid on trays and fertiliser bags
and leaves of rustling bracken until,
our fingers twined, into another age we spilled!

A Drop In The Ocean

David Kemp

KITTY'S grandad had been a sailor in his time. "I've wrung more salt water out of my sea-boot socks than you'll ever sail over," he was fond of telling the kids. He'd started out with the fishing, been deep sea, gone foreign, and finally washed ashore in a tiny cottage down on the Cape, swallowed the anchor after a lifetime at sea.

"Best thing about boats is watching them buggers float past," he'd say, tucked up in his cubby on a wild Sunday afternoon, while the squalls rattled the salt-caked windows that looked west over the Brisons.

The room was snug and filled with tacka tack, sailor's swag from Mombasa to Martinique. Framed photos of ships he had sailed shared shelf space with a Christ in a snowstorm from Rio, and carved seashells from the Seychelles. The kids loved his display of keepsakes and old Billy had a story that went with each one of them.

"Got that dagger in Baghdad when you was still in your dad's bag," he'd say, pointing out some dusty relic hidden in a dark corner.

But the strangest story he ever told was connected to a very ordinary-looking bottle he kept in a polished wooden box by his armchair. The box was hand-made and lined with green felt. The bottle looked like an old jam jar. It had a sealed top, and seemed to be filled with a clear liquid, perhaps water.

"Yes, and water is 'zackly what's in it," he declared, holding the bottle up to the light. "I've sailed over a few trillion gallons of the stuff, and probably some of it more than once."

It has been claimed that every breath we take contains at least one molecule of air once expelled from the lungs of the emperor Caesar, and Billy firmly believed that H_2O shared the same characteristics.

"It's what they call the 'water cycle'," he'd explain. "Starts somewhere, maybe the ocean, goes up into the sky, falls as rain, eats mountains. On its return to the sea it passes through the intestines of fish, falls as tears from the eyes of the prophet, flows through garden hoses en route. The cycle goes on and on, repeating for aeons, so that tiny droplets shaken from a harpy's wing will eventually turn up again, perhaps mixed with milk and sugar in this very pot of tea we are now sharing. Yep, water goes on forever, but this particular bottle here," – he'd tap it significantly with his forefinger – "ain't changed hardly at all since I sealed it up sixty years ago."

The jar, he said, he'd had a little longer. His mother would fill it up with homemade spicy lozenges, sealed watertight to keep him warm on a cold dark night's fishing. You can buy them all bagged up and called *Fisherman's Friends* nowadays.

"I was a junior hand on a lugger in them days. We'd go deep sea after them pisces, and when the wind was right, sail well out of sight of the land. Anyhow, we was out there bobbing about one misty night, waiting to haul in, when just then we see this gigantic vessel bearing down on us out of the fog. She couldn't see us from on top of them iron walls and was nearly upon us. I hauled in the sheet to bear round, but the block was tangled. I scrambled up the mast to free the sail just as she struck, them mighty bows crunching our little boat like a welly boot scrunching a wood louse. Being on top of the mast, I was flicked, like an ink pellet off a ruler, high into the air. I remember spinning past a towering cliff of steel, black as night, with rivets for stars, tumbling over and over in a wide arc past rows of blazing portholes, a clunk on the back of my head, then nothing more.

"Some time later – I couldn't say how long, hours, more like days, I suspect – I came to. I'd struck my head and was hazy and confused. I lay in a coma for at least another day and night, 'til I came to my senses and was able to look around me. Incredibly, it seemed that I'd been flicked so high into the air, that I had fallen back on to the boat deck of the very vessel that had struck us. I was lying cradled in the canvas cover of a lifeboat that had softened my fall. It was night-time, and I had come round enough to clamber out of the boat. I stood leaning on the ship's rail, bleary and wobbly, trying to get my balance whilst my eyes tried to focus on the water far below. Suddenly an enormous white shape loomed out of the darkness. There was a series of lurching groans and shudders, and I was pitched forward over the rail on to the cold hard surface of an iceberg, as it ground along the ship's side. In a moment, the upper decks of the vessel had glided past me, and I lifted my head to see the huge liner, lights ablaze, drift slowly astern, disappearing into the darkness.

"The first few hours on the iceberg were not completely silent. I can remember the shouts, the screams, the hiss of escaping steam as the vessel sunk. For a while there were the dreadful cries of the survivors, then silence, and later on, the calls from searching rescue vessels. No one thought of looking up on the top of the mighty iceberg, where I sat marooned on my icy throne.

"After a few days, we drifted away from the debris, floating southwards. I was well wrapped up and quite used to being alone at sea, but getting very hungry. All that I had in the pockets of my oilskins was a bit of smoked mackerel, which I soon gnawed, and this jar, which was still full of them spicy lozenges me mother had given me. As we drifted south into warmer seas, the berg began to melt.

"Or maybe it was weeping. For amongst all that ice there must have been the frozen tears of angels, which started to flow for all them poor souls that had been lost. Yes, for although much of an iceberg is submerged and hidden, deep down they can have feelings too. They can only take so much, and after such an enormous collision, this one had started to crack up."

Billy kept it together though, and as he was swept slowly southwards, he kept himself warm with charitable thoughts and nourished himself with his bottle of lozenges, one spicy sweet twice a day, at sunrise and sun-set. As he took each lozenge from the bottle, he would replace it with a chunk of ice, and put the bottle back inside his oilskins, in his breast pocket.

By the time he'd reached the Tropics, he'd scoffed the lot, and was left only with a bottle of warm sugary water for nourishment. The berg had shrunk to a tiny shadow of its former self, and Billy sat astride a chunk of ice, barely a metre above the water, surrounded by a pack of hungry sharks, waiting for their dinner to defrost.

The steamer was a day out of Curacao, bound for Lobito, when they picked him up, ranting about proper job pasties and clutching his bottle. He stayed with them until Durban and then signed on a tramp bound for Liverpool – via the Antipodes. It wasn't until after the war that he finally made a landfall off the coast of Cornwall again. Jumping ship at Falmouth, he made his way back home.

What with the war, and the mines, things had changed much for the worse at St Just. There were many more who had disappeared since his lugger went down, and most of them would never return. He told his story once or twice, but folk had lost so much it didn't seem right to brag about his own incredible luck when time had run right out for so many of his mates.

Last winter Billy slipped his moorings for the last time, and set out on the big voyage. They put his remains in a box and burnt it, then sprinkled his ashes off the Brisons. He's part of the blue Gulf Stream now, except for the bits on their way north to the icebergs again.

We went round to clear up his house last week. A lifetime's bits and bobs had been packed into plastic fish crates by his niece, and most of it bound for the car boot sale. She had taken what she wanted and left us to help ourselves.

In a Tesco bag, I found the box. The bottle had been opened and all but a gulp, gone. It seems that Billy had taken a few swigs to sustain himself on his last trip outward bound. Left in the bottom of the bottle, there was only one inch of melt-water left from the iceberg that sunk the Titanic. Now, who would swallow that?

Moored Up

Liz Harman

My Jan, you know, has retired,
Given up the sea-going life,
And I thank the Lord the time has come
I'm no longer a fisherman's wife.
No more must I heed the gale warnings,
No longer endure the dread fog,
For he's there in his chair by the fire,
"Jan, my 'ansum, throw on a fresh log."
The watching, the waiting and hoping he's safe
Are no longer things to fear,
For my dear man has come ashore,
He's fastened to the pier.
No doubt time will come when he's under my feet,
That I'll wish he was back at sea,
Then I'll think of him coming home tired and grey
And be thankful he's right here with me.
For I mind the times that he's come ashore
Almost too weary to stand,
When the trip has been bad, with torn nets and lost gear
And they've only just made land.
So I say to the girl who proposes
To marry a seagoing man,
You're going to need courage and patience and strength
And love him all you can.
But now my Jan I have landed,
He is tied up good and fast,
And the years that remain promise comfort and peace
Because I've got him anchored at last.

The Perfect Cornish Christmas

Jane Nancarrow

THE snow was deep that Christmas. We crunched up Tredydan Road, with noses as red as cherries, dragging our ancient home-made sledges. Relics! The waterfall by the forge was frozen, and so was Bates' pond. We loved its cold smoothness as it shone in the pale, gleaming, wintry sunlight.

In the frost-covered field, Herbie's old grey horse stood like a statue. Its breath froze in the cold air. We climbed over the rickety gate, praying that the spinsters in the small row of houses opposite would not be peering at us through their yellowing, lace curtains. Our fingers burned on the frosted gate.

Then up into Stacey's field, across the pure Arctic wastes of virgin snow. Breath coming in vapourous pants, noses dripping, fingers blue despite our itchy woollen gloves and sodden sheepskin mittens. We puffed up the hill, ridge after ridge. Trees silhouetted against a bleak winter's sky.

It was Christmas Eve. We threw snowballs and sledged, while the sun sank into a rosy glow. We were cold, wet, but happy, as we dragged our wood-wormed sledges home. We sang as we trudged down the road, past the darkening pond.

"Silent Night. Holy Night."

Great-Aunt Vi's favourite, ringing out with an innocence, clearly, over the white fields of snow, now shadowed with deepening blue. We crunched home, satisfied, back to the flickering firelight and tingling toes. Back to our harassed mothers, wrestling with the goose-bumped flesh of poultry in sage-and-onion sculleries, back to the boiling of hams and the smells of cinnamon and saffron mingling with the musty smell of little-used front rooms (or parlours as the older folk called them).

Balloons floated mysteriously in corners, home-made paper streamers decked the ceilings and the pine-scented Christmas tree stood proudly in its bucket of earth, ready for decorating.

Boxes of faded decorations were brought up the stone steps from the dark, spidery cellar. Soon the tree glittered with tinsel and fragile glass baubles. Crepe paper adorned the tin bucket. Small, spiralling candles lit up the pine boughs, dramatically. We sensed the danger! Family portraits of long-gone weddings were adorned with the dark green of holly and mistletoe.

Late on Christmas Eve we ventured out into the white wilderness, bound for the midnight mass. Above us, the moon sailed across a clear sky, and sheep bleated plaintively in the higher fields.

Launceston Castle glowered down on us as it reflected on hundreds of Christmases past. Time and nature held us in its icy grip. We slid down the hill, past the town mill. Snow flew like flour in the darkness. We slid and skidded our way down to the river. It swirled past, black and oily, under the pack-horse bridge.

The church bells rang out, raggedly at first, into the stillness. We shivered with anticipation. The mystery of Christmas was about to unfold.

On this very night, the beasts in the stable at Bethlehem had fallen to their knees before the Christ-child.

So, into the vestry, breath smoking in the night air, we dragged on our cassocks, damp against the boys' white cotton shirts.

The church was bathed in mellow candle-light. Stone faces leered at us in the shadows from the Norman font. The pews were packed with people for their Christmas communion.

The organ creaked its introduction. The choir cleared its communal throat and launched into the first carol, to its old Cornish tune.

"*While shepherds washed their socks by night,*" we mouthed irreverently.

The candles flickered in the draughts, my grandfather's tenor soared out across the chancel, snow fell in the darkness outside.

God was in his Heaven.

All was right with the world.

Tomorrow would be Christmas Day.

In Praise Of
Living Cornwall

Ann Trevenen Jenkin

Blackberries, rocks, water,
Little homesteads, OK pasties.

Saffron cake, heavy cake too,
A pint of beer, wine or milk.

Ice-cream and red strawberries –
Food I do love a thousandfold.

The history of Cornwall, vigorously taught,
The Men-an-Tol, an ancient dolmen.

A church, wells, a very holy cross,
Sea, sand dunes, river and valley.

The ancient names, Moyle, Polglase,
Piran, Tamsyn, greatly honoured.

The Cornish flag, white and black,
The Cornish tongue, thanks be to God.

The people of Cornwall, strong our voice,
The spirit of Cornwall, living and powerful.

Ow-Cormola
Bewnans Kernow

Ann Trevenen Jenkin

Moren du, carrygy, dowr,
Trevow byghan, pastyow lowr.

Tesen Saffern, hevva ynweth,
Pynta coref, gwyn po leth.

Dehen rew ha syvy ruth –
Bos y-garaf-vy, mylwyth.

Ystory Kernewek, dyskys yn-fen,
Men and Tol ha dolmen hen.

Eglos, pythow, crows pur sans,
Mor, tewennow, avon, nans.

Hynwyn cothow, Moyl, Ploglas,
Pyran, Tamsyn, mur dhe les.

Baner Kernow, gwyn ha du,
Yeth Kernewek, gras dhe Dhew.

Pobel Kernow men agan lef,
Enef Kernow, bew ha cref.

A Message Of Bells

Bert Biscoe

Up Trurrer 'tis Sunday;
first Sabbath of December,
and Boscawen Street
is twinklin' like a carnival,
and the bells of St Mary's
are swingin' and ringin',
and makin' the hearts leap
in shop-struck children.
Over 'ere, St Keverne way,
'pon the slip of a nor'easterly breeze,
we, Flamanck 'n me,
perpetually bronzed and planted 'ere,
can hear they bells soundin' out
and in the echoes between their strikes,
as the ropes slide through sally-catch hands,
bronze to bronze they d'cry:
Stand straight, mind! Say yer piece!
'Tis only just begun! 'Tis only begun!
And in the cruel teeth of winter's jaws,
Clench yer fist, boys! Spring will come!

Crosbie Garstin
~ A Cornish Mystery
Michael Williams

CROSBIE Garstin's place in Cornish literature is secure. Elephant Bill, who knew him well, said of Garstin: "No man affected my life more. He instilled in me, as a boy, the spirit of wanderlust and of going places and doing things and seeing things long before he became an author."

No more colourful, more imaginative storyteller emerged from Cornwall between the wars. Crosbie Garstin's reputation rests firmly on his Penhale trilogy. They have such visual quality, and what a cinema film or television series they would make.

First came *The Owl's House*. I never enter the Angel Hotel at Helston without thinking of that brilliant opening chapter – John Penhale with his badly scarred face to the wall. This was followed by *High Noon* and finally *The West Wind*, dedicated to "Norman Garstin, dearest of fathers, wittiest of companions, best of friends".

The irony of the Penhale trilogy was that he set out to write a single novel. In the original final chapter of *The Owl's House* Penhale died, but his publisher, Heinmann, telegrammed: "Rewrite last chapter. Penhale too good a character to kill off!"

There were other works, among them *The Mudlarks*, *The Dragon & The Lotus*, which he illustrated (he was an excellent cartoonist), *Vagabond Verses* and *Samuel Kelly, An 18th Century Seaman*, which he edited and in which he wrote five perceptive pages of introduction.

To begin at the beginning, Crosbie Garstin was born

on 7th May 1887 in a house in Alexandra Road, Penzance, close to the Pirates rugby ground. His father Norman was a painter and an important pioneer in the creation of Newlyn as an artists' colony. His mother was half Welsh, half English.

The tragedy is Crosbie Garstin died, aged only 43. Further fame and fortune surely lay ahead. There must have been more stories and books inside this larger than life character, a man who might have been thinly disguised in an Ernest Hemingway novel.

It was a sailing invitation to join the Holman family that led to the tragedy. Miss Olive Wesley, who typed many of his manuscripts and ran a typing school in South Parade, Penzance, told me that he insisted on getting his novel typed and away to the publishers before finally accepting the invitation.

"He was working at tremendous pressure to finish *The West Wind*," she recalled. "And in a strange sort of way I blame myself for his death in that I typed into the early hours of the morning so that the novel could be sent to London."

Typing finished, and manuscript posted, Garstin joined the Holmans on their yacht. At Salcombe, on the first night, however, he felt tired and said he would not join the others who were going ashore to a party. Later in the evening he became bored, changed his mind and went ashore. And much later in the evening he and a young lady in a fur coat, together with another person, set out for the yacht in a pram – a small boat that normally carries only two passengers. A short distance from the shore, in total darkness, the pram began to sink. The third member of the party swam back to the shore for help, while the young lady later admitted that she owed her life to the fact that "invisible hands" removed her fur coat and helped her to get back to land. In the process of saving her life, Crosbie Garstin lost his own. Drama and mystery deepened in that his body was never found.

I interviewed his widow, Lilian Garstin, a one-time Mayor of Penzance, and met his sister Alethea, an accomplished painter, on four or five occasions, including a visit to her house, with stunning views across the green-grey Zennor landscape.

In 1981 I wrote about Crosbie Garstin in a book called *Strange Happenings In Cornwall* and, in the context of his strange death, reflected: "At the time some people thought Garstin had vanished into thin air – to make a new start elsewhere."

Others later saw an uncanny prophecy in his last paragraph, written probably only hours or, at most, days before his death and disappearance. In the Epilogue of that last published novel, he wrote: "Anthony Penhale sat motionless for a long while in thought. Then rising, he kissed the happy face and went downstairs to tell his wife that all was over – or all beginning."

Was it all over? Or was there a new beginning?

It was in July 1988 that the Crosbie Garstin story – for me – took a remarkable twist. A clergyman, the Reverend David Dewey BA MSc, from Enfield in Middlesex, decided to write to me.

Here is what he had to say in his letter:

"My wife and I have just returned from a visit to Cornwall during which we bought a copy of your most interesting book. I was particularly interested in your account of the mysterious disappearance of Crosbie Garstin in that I might be able to shed some light on the matter. In the year 1960 I worked for a short time in the office of a South London firm. There was already a Mr Garstin employed there. He left the firm a few months later but he did tell me a little about himself.

"He was a Roman Catholic, a pipe smoker and had

served in World War I, where he had won a commission in the field. Furthermore he told me he had been an author who had written under the names of Crosbie Garstin, John Crosbie and Norman Leslie. Under the latter name he had published whodunits. At about that time I found in my local library a book entitled, *The Owl's House*, by Crosbie Garstin. I mentioned this discovery to Mr Garstin, who acknowledged his authorship of the book.

"He seemed to me to be a man of good upbringing, although a rather sad and lonely individual. He spoke once of no longer having a home of his own; indeed he was living, at that time, in rooms in Clapham.

"Unless there are two novelists of the same name it would seem that Crosbie Garstin was alive and well in 1960. It is unlikely that he is alive today.

"On the face of it, it does not look as though he died whilst saving the life of a young lady.

"Obviously you know far more about this strange story than I, but I can assure you, as a clergyman, that what I have told is true. It is at least another piece in the Cornish jigsaw."

Recently I talked again with David Dewey – our first conversation since 1988 – and he still had a crystal-clear memory of his former work colleague.

"Mr Garstin, we called him that in the office, had come down in the world, working as a clerk for a wholesale grocery business. I'd say he was then a man of 70. I remember he wore beautiful expensive shoes, a legacy of his more prosperous days. Not the kind of shoes you'd expect to find a clerk wearing."

So, Crosbie Garstin's life beyond that night at Salcombe remains a mystery.

Trevor's Kiss
Michael Sagar Fenton

W HEN I woke up Rael was bending over my bunk, shaking me. I sat straight up, stiff and cold. "Is clear," he said. Outside the wooden shack the morning mist was still thick and damp, but looking up I could see that there were patches of blue breaking through. The clouds had wrapped our mountain for three endless days, cold soaking curtains which left us all huddling around the iron stove. Rael nodded to me, his intelligent face creased in its habitual frown.

"Today, Trevor's Kiss."

Christo fried some bacon which we ate with rye-bread rolls and tea. There was little gear to pack, since this was only a scouting trip and not a fully-fledged expedition. I took only my normal case, which I let Christo carry since there was no other use for his stocky shoulders. He seemed anxious, as if I would not pay him, but the wide smile never left his brown face. He spoke no English.

"Propadee!" he said. "Balge knee!"

"He's excited," I said to Rael.

"Yes," he said. "Christo found this place. Many bat. No one see before."

Bats were my current concern. I was scouting for a wildlife film unit, and had a few weeks to search the mountains for the most photogenic bat caves. Like most wild areas of the world I had found it too well-travelled already, everything known, seen and catalogued. But not "Trevor's Kiss". No one but Christo had seen it for many years, and no one I spoke to had ever heard of it.

We piled into the old blue Land-Rover and set off up the steep shale track. Below us the lower peaks were pushing through the mist into the sunshine, which was already hurtingly bright. The track went through scrubby bushes for several miles before climbing a series of steep zig-zags.

At the top of the ridge I expected a valley or another climb, but instead there was a small plateau on which sat a beautiful lake. It lay without a ripple like a sheet of stainless steel, surrounded by a green thicket, faithfully reversing the mountains which climbed on upwards, the snowy peaks nearest to our eyes. The track led by the lake, not to it, and stopped in a rough circle.

"Can we go to the lake?"

Rael shook his head.

"Much bite," he said.

Of course. Bats did not live on nothing. I set up the tripod and took some photographs. Christo was impatient.

"Come," he said, fidgeting and pacing. "Come. Propadee. Trevor's Kiss."

I packed up and Christo took my case once more. We set off up a steep path, which stopped at the stream that fed the lake. There was a clear pool, and we all drank the freezing water. I looked around, unable to see where to go next. Christo saw me looking and mocked my efforts, pantomiming looking around with his dark brown eyes, left and right, which way? His smile split even wider as he jumped on to a rock and started climbing up the stream-bed itself.

"Come."

There were enough rocks to keep our feet out of the water, though the climb took away my breath in the thin air. Soon I was panting.

"Can we rest? Is it far?"

"Rest." said Rael. "Not long."

I sat on the cold stone while Christo foraged away upstream and Rael stood like a tree, his tall figure hunched over. I looked around. The mist had all burned away and the mountains were sharply beautiful. I could see the threads of streams in the deep valleys, the wooded hillsides, the bare uplands, the snowy peaks receding into haze. The silence was a presence, broken only by the occasional call of a kite, far above. Heat soon turned to cold, and I shivered.

"Trevor's Kiss – was it made by man?"

Rael nodded.

"A mine?"

"Small," said Rael.

"What would anyone mine up here?"

Christo was back and seemed to understand my question.

"Silva," he said.

I hoped the miner had found plenty. What else could drive a man to live and work in such utter remoteness?

"Spanish?"

"English," said Rael.

"English," said Christo. "Balge knee. Propadee."

I turned to Rael, but he only shrugged.

We left the stream-bed at last and tracked across a scree slope on a barely-discernible path. It led to a further tumble of bare rocks, and I looked for a way up. But there was no need. Christo dropped my case and scampered ahead, beckoning us around the side of a huge boulder.

"Trevor's Kiss," he declared.

The hole was not natural, perhaps a fissure worked by hand into an almost square entrance, four feet or so high. Inside was dark as night, but the pile of droppings outside and the characteristic smell told of a medium-sized colony.

I went to the entrance, looking immediately outwards, not in. I was imagining the show the bats would make as they poured out of this hole at dusk like smoke from burning oil.

Disappointment soaked into me. The colony was fine and the setting was good, but the arrangement of the rocks left no clear camera angle. The bats would have to climb up almost at once and disperse out of sight. What happened here every night had all been seen before, and better. In the competitive world of natural history filming, novelty was the only currency.

"See bat!"

Christo was almost dancing with pride. I assumed a look of delight and took the torch he was handing me.

The mine was not deep inside, fifty or sixty yards, stopping at a sheer face. It was higher inside where the crack worked up through the entrails of the mountain. The bats rustled overhead, and the smell was almost tangible. The colony was well-established. Had the forgotten miner worked amongst them, or had he scared them away, only for them to return when he stumbled, defeated, back down the mountain? There were no human objects to tell the tale, no clues at all.

I came out again and put to Rael the question I had waited patiently to ask.

"Why Trevor's Kiss?"

He spoke to Christo in his own language, and in answer Christo led us again to the mine entrance. He took out his knife and scratched the blunt side against a rock on the right-hand side. It was large and triangular, a reverse pyramid.

Under the covering of dried stray droppings there were marks in the rock, and as I watched, letters formed beneath his knife. I stood still as he scraped away, cold seeping through my body. Christo finished his work and stood proudly back. He smiled broadly, then stared uncertainly as he saw my face.

"You know?" said Rael.

"I know," I said, hardly trusting my voice. I too was far from home. The letters fitted crudely into the shape of the stone were a labour of love, a work of many evenings with hammer and chisel around the fire after a hard day at the rock face. They spelt:

BAL JENNY

PROP.D.

TREVAS-

KIS

There was a pride in it. At the top of the world was a place where he had at least been owned by no master. It was his own enterprise. One mountain, one Cornishman, and only hard work and good fortune to determine the outcome.

"Is good?" said Rael.

"Yes," I said. "It was a man from my own country."

"England," he said.

"Yes," I said. "Near England."

I took photographs of the mine to please the others, and some of the inscription to take home with me.

Below, the light was already slanting, and purple shadows hid the valley floor. Silently we started back down the mountain.

Roscommon
Katharine Grey

I flee from fireside, out into the night,
Stumbling on granite, sent to trap my foot.
I look for nothingness, clutching at space,
And it engulfs me, greater than my mood.

The air is wild and reckless, malevolent,
Battering the little garden with its scrubby trees.
The eucalyptus swings and cringes by the house,
And the wind claws at every tile and stone.

My face braces itself: I cannot see. Then
I stare blindly into spattered clouds
Like spume, which blast with hail and rain
Tired beasts that lean unseen against a wall.

And far away across the blackness, hear
The distant rush and ebb of timeless tides
Groan and sigh like some vast multitude,
As slamming seas crash into indifferent rocks.

Above the cliffs, the ancient farmstead stands,
Invisible, invincible beyond the ragged fields,
One light alone, in all that awesome dark,
Roscommon hangs like hope in endless night.

Skin
Chantal Brooks

I AM in a maze with secret passageways twisting and disappearing in front of me. The hedges are too high to peer over, but every now and again, in between the densely planted shrubs, I can see feet running, a child's feet in black patent leather shoes.

She is as lost as I am; I only see the reflection of myself in a mirror as I run towards it, the same mirror I ran away from years ago. I know that this is the same mirror because it is on the back of my wardrobe door, the same wardrobe that I had as a child. So I've returned to the place that I started from, like I had been stuck in a revolving door for the past thirty years.

My dead father brought me back to this village, into this house that is nestled beside a slipstream of traffic, in a cleft which dips between two breasts of granite hillside. My dead father that came and whispered into my ear as I slept and when I doubted my dreams he left little signs, the same signs we had used when I was a child.

A tower of stones, an arrow shaped from branches, a black cat running across my pathway. This is the way I found myself back at the beginning again.

It is autumn, I feel the air changing; appropriate really. My life is changing with the wind. I have shed an old skin like leaves and grown another. My old skin was full of callouses, hard layers building up over the years. My belly was covered in molluscs and crustaceans – you tend to get these if you swim against the tide. I grew weary and the currents were much too strong. I started peeling, my skin became segmented, blistering like an orange; it was dry and became sour. I would wake in the morning to the sound of rustling, gather up my sheets into a bundle and walk outside to shake them out. The wind would take the flakes of dead skin dancing across the garden into the hedge, some catching another blast, carrying them faster and higher, eddying up past the launders, up past the roof.

I began to wonder if I would grow moth wings but I think that was because of the colour and the fine dust, which floated around the room and was caught in the shafts of early morning sunlight. It's the luck of the draw what flesh you metamorphose into. Some people have told me that they itched for a fortnight, others of how wet and slimy they felt and the odd smell of lemons.

When my new skin began it was beautiful. It was smooth and warm, a mesh of fine chain-mail, silver and iridescent.

The colour changes with the heat of my body. In the bitter winds of winter I am the colour of a rare pearl and in the blazing heat of summer I shimmer an emerald green. This is a fine skin, very delicate and so thin it is translucent.

I begin to grow impatient, I want to know why I am back here and why my beautiful skin is as thin as paper. This makes me feel so vulnerable. I don't tell my dead father this, but I think he knows. He tells me to wait. So I wait.

One evening when I am out walking to pass the time of waiting I meet a man who knows my name, and I talk to him out of politeness. I do not recognise this man's face or body but I do recognise his eyes and the way he tilts his head, and I know the time of waiting has passed. He has a dead father who is silent or maybe he just doesn't hear.

There is no stillness in his life; he runs barefoot through his maze across broken glass, he sacrifices himself for others because he doesn't know how to shed his skin.

The patterns of the fine chain-mail upon my skin can be read like a map so that he can find his way home. But he doesn't read maps.

I am cutting strands of my hair to bind his heart. It is like fine gold thread that won't break. I am wrapping him in my body, within my skin to heal his wounds. I am sharing the heat of my flesh to colour his skin.

I am washing his feet with my tears and kiss them to stop them bleeding.

He is a man but he is as delicate as glass – if I drop him he will shatter. He holds me in his hand.

My skin is delicate, it is fragile, it is all I have. The more I give to him the more transparent it becomes.

I risk everything to stop him in his tracks, to stop him running through his maze, to bring stillness; to kiss his face with gentleness and to hold him tenderly.

He takes my hand and shows me his maze, our reflections caught this time by the water in a fish pond. It is a reflection of a young girl wearing black patent leather shoes and a boy in whose eyes I can see my reflection. I like the way he tilts his head.

It is easier to remember him as a boy than to see him as this man. Behind those eyes he has changed and I know this is the turning point. My skin feels taut, and although it is not marked I think that if anyone touches me it will burn.

I have started to lose my colour and soon I will be colourless, almost invisible. The man wears his hurt and self-pity like symbols of great strength. When I see this man and feel his skin, the scars read like Braille.

Beneath his chest and aching ribs, where he has been running so fast trying to flee and trying to stay, I feel his heart pounding, pierced with shards of glass and initials etched deeply into his heart. They are not my initials. I am tired and all the while ache for something more. My sighs are plenty and deep, tremors from my soul, making my whole body shake. The man thinks that maybe I am unhappy and have been crying. It is my soul sobbing, telling me to come home.

The reflection in the fish pond is still, even though tiny periwinkle shells break the surface of the water. When I look in I can only see yellow stars in my hair. I trace a line with my finger over the water and watch fishes dart between the rocks. I cup my hands and scoop up the mother-of-pearl liquid. I hold it high, it refracts the sun, a million suns. It runs down my arms and soothes my skin. This is the beginning, this is when I know that I am going home.

I live now in between the ebb and flow. I watch the seas swallow a melting sun and the moon with an opal halo of rain clouds. I wear a filigree of kelp and bladder wrack. Starfish swim in my hair, which has grown back longer and softer.

Every velvet night under the scattered light of the crystal stars I swim with horses as they roll and kick in the surf, eyes wild and nostrils flared. I wrap my arms around their necks and listen to them breathe. As we break the surface they whinny and toss their heads and lunge like the carved painted horses of the fairground. Under the sea, in the moonlight we are pale, the colour of mottled marble. I lay on their backs and feel their hearts pounding; every sinew in their bodies is taut. As I dive underneath their bellies and watch their legs kicking, streams of bubbles and phosphorescence rise to the surface. With tightened muscles and flanks of water they gallop up on to the sands and then roll back into the depths.

Moving slowly through the dark fathoms, timeless,

ageless, like a wave, that gentle motion lulling, Leviathan and calf, the grain of the sea, their song calls to me, reaches into my heart and pulls me closer. A beam of light swings around from the lighthouse to find only emptiness on the indigo black waters of the ocean. In the morning light, strangers come in glass-bottomed boats to see if they can catch a glimpse of my radiant skin, diving under the snakeskin water. I am well-known, a myth, a legend. I swim with the tide now; the longer I swim, the sleeker, faster, lighter I become.

I am in my element. From my heart and soul where the sobbing started resonates a light so strong that when I open my mouth to let it out, it spills out in song. Crowds come to listen to this sound that is so beguiling; it makes hearts break or stop beating and breath to be stilled.

Out in the vast stretches of the Baltic seas or the balmy Indian Ocean or the storm driven Atlantic, I sing. As my voice weaves in between the legs of the oil platforms and echoes through the steel corridors of the whaling ships and the tankers the size of floating cities my song haunts the sailors' minds.

I call their souls back home to the seas. Men close their eyes and cry at my song and leave behind leather purses filled with gold coins and sweethearts filled with babies.

They stir in the darkness of their dreams and come to the water's edge, whole villages sometimes, to listen to the song of their soul calling them home.

Marcheug Ann Tonnow

Tim Saunders

for Marc Gajardo

Glew ha' glan
marc'heug ow' troezya mordan,
c'hwaré ow' tava tyweuz:
galar a'veudh yn y gan.

Soen ha' si
huz gwynz ow' kanna heli:
 tonn mîlweîth ow' rÿi taveuz
a'vrath morrebow a vri.

Hael y hudh
ow' fetha keudh ha' kÿstudh:
pyw a'vydh nefra pareuz
dhÿ goll tywl ha' gwoeyow rudh?

Worth kwrr ann byz, kov glas koll fell
a'blymm ganz nell dre Fystral ann bryz:
gwaneg y spyryz a'wolc'h ann traeth pell.

Knight Of The Waves

Tim Saunders

for Marc Gajardo

Clearly and brightly a knight treads phosphorescence,
soon to touch sand: pain will drown in his song.

The spell and the hum of wind's magic bleaches seawa-
ter: a wave gives voice a thousand times and will bite
into shores of renown.

With his generous merriment he will conquer sorrow and
confusion: who will ever be prepared for dark loss and
red woes?

On the other side of the world, the green memory of
cruel loss will billow energetically through the mind's
Fistral: the breaker of his spirit will wash the distant
shore.

Dreaming Of Brief Encounters

Marie Macneill

Shut out that pack of wolves –
Those demanding thin grey-suited men,
And people with their me-me whines –
Who howl and bark and bay for blood.
Don't answer the bell, the fax, the phone –
They only ring to wring you dry. Instead
Just shut your eyes. And dream.
Perhaps of foolish days on windswept dunes
Watching blood-red suns dive and die.
Or moonlight dancing on winking waves –
Your footprints on the tide.
Or quiet rivers where the salmon leap –
And willows kiss meandering flow.
Or maybe a plane tree as it bends and sways
Above two lovers, on some secret tryst,
Or blazing eyes in ash fire glow,
That sparkle warm with wine and lust,
The haplessness of friendship –
And a simple word called trust.
Think too of silk soft skin, an arching back, an aching limb,
An inner thigh, a thrusting moan, a hungry mouth –
Now you're home. Her ruffled smile, your tousled grin,
Jump into that moonlit dream. And linger for a while.
And when those men, with daggers bright
Dull the sword of truth –
Draw up her blanket of a thousand smiles
Wrap it round and warm. Stay awake, and watch the night
Breaking into dawn.

On Bolenowe Crofts

Dennis Gould

for John Harris

On Bolenowe Crofts stand long-empty cottages,
Engine-houses, shafts silent as tombstones,
Wheal Grenville crumbles into schoolbooks,
Red River rises up the valley below Nine Maidens,
Fox and badger creep through Four Lanes village,
In the sky more helicopters than hawks,
Some mushrooms and blackberries not yet killed off
By short-term fertilisers. Uncle Ned's rock has
Few lovers meeting now where once they jellyrolled
In long grass well-hidden from ageing ones frowning.
Few holidaymakers glance up at passing pilots
In training as squadron leaders of airfleet gunships,
Metallic birds of prey drowning screams of ecstasy
In passing flooded mines and ghost railways.
Immigrants and emigrants, colony of wealth poverty-ridden,
China clay millionaires sitting on empty cottage
Property, buying up land regularly, potter's wheels,
Fishermen's nets, mounds of scrap iron dereliction,
Crab-apple Methodism fearful of fun and dance music,
Mutual aid and joyful thoughtful anarchy,
Goonhilly-eared duke farting out monarchy's rights
Unaware of long-haired poets and lovers hardthinking.

The World Is
The Same Place

Pauline Sheppard
March 20 2003

Your sand doesn't look like this.
My friends come over the dune,
Arab-scarfed
against sand-blasting wind;
their cries are whipped
from my ears.
I can see their eyes.
They stare
at the white sand shore
to see
what the chemical waves wash up:
chalky skins sucked clean
from calcified skeletons,
weed like the head of Pen Glaz,
the life-bringer,
tossed on the foaming manes
of Tresco waves.
It rains on the deserts,
and my sand,
my holiday sand,
will kiss the cheeks of my enemies,
arab-scarfed
against the sand-blasting wind,
in another country
in the same place.

Notes On The Contributors

Bert Biscoe is rooted and versed in Cornwall. In his youth he wrote songs, played guitar and toured in a succession of bands, before immersing himself in the cultural development and politics of Cornwall. Chairman of the Cornish Constitutional Convention – the campaign to establish a directly elected regional assembly of Cornwall – he is a poet and Bard of the Gorsedd, whose published collections include *Words Of Granite*, *Accompanied By Larks*, and *At A Wedding With Yeats In Turin*.

Chantal Brooks has been writing since "my first gold star for a poem at Lanner infants school". She took it up again seriously ten years ago. She is currently working on a collection of short stories and a novel, *Various Envies*. She lives in Camborne and has three teenage children.

Paul Farmer is a writer, performer and film maker. A Bard of the Gorsedd, he is a founder of A39 Theatre and Scavel An Gow. He has written and directed films in both English and Kernewek. He lives in Playing Place.

Dennis Gould is a poet, cyclist, peace activist and footballer. He founded *Riff/Raff Poets* at St Ives Festival in 1970, and *Whisper And Shout*. While living in the cottage where poet and miner John Harris was born, at Six Chimneys, he ran a radical Redruth book shop and became an inspiration to disaffected Cornish youth. His published work includes *Redruth Days*. He makes postcards and posterpoems using a traditional letterpress.

Martin Green is a poet and author who has lived in and out of Newlyn for the past 20 years. He has written guides to London pubs, a book about traditional customs and a number of poetry collections. These include his versions of work by 14th century Welsh poet Dafydd ap Gwilym, an elegy for the dead of the Spanish Civil War and his latest, *A Night With Fiona Pitt-Kethley*.

Katharine Grey lives on a windswept smallholding in the far west of Cornwall, where she grows plants and trees. She works as a researcher and proof-reader, makes ceramic pots and writes poetry.

Carl Grose was born in Truro, and has been lucky enough to live and work in Cornwall at the same time. In 1995, he joined Kneehigh Theatre and has worked extensively with them ever since, appearing in such shows as *Wolf*, *Pandora's Box* and *The King Of Prussia*. His own writing includes *Quick Silver* (Kneehigh), *The Eclipse Play* (Grinning Gargoyle), *Scorched* (o-region) and *Boris Bitty's Brand New Parents* (BBC TV). He is currently writing two screenplays about growing up in Cornwall. *Dead Man's Fingers* was recorded at Falmouth Maritime Museum and broadcast on Radio 3.

Stacey Guthrie is a mental health support worker. Born and educated in Penzance, she lives on a five-acre smallholding in Nancledra with her husband and three sons. *Helga's Gone Abroad* is about her alter-ego, Helga the Hormonal, a pre-menstrual Valkyrie who the populace of Penzance have voted Mock Mayor on several occasions during the annual Golowan festival. Needless to say, a Hormonal Valkyrie finds understanding the human race somewhat of a challenge

Stephen Hall is a Madron man, having lived in Penwith for all of his fifty-four years, except for a brief foray to London and seven years in County Kerry. Stephen created the Penwith Community Archive, co-wrote and toured

Duffy And The Devil, and helped to revive the Golowan Festival and Trust, of which he is director. Writer, songwriter, musician and traditional singer, he is a founder member of Scavel An Gow and a Bard of the Gorsedd.

Des Hannigan lives in West Cornwall and is a writer and photographer, working mainly on travel books. He has written guides to Northern Europe, Denmark, Andalucía, Corfu, Rhodes and North Pakistan and is a main author of Lonely Planet's new editions of Ireland and Greece. In a previous century he was a share fisherman for 15 years. He says it was "an easier life".

Liz Harman was born in Newlyn and, apart from four years of "exile" in Penzance, has lived there all her life. She started writing poems and stories many years ago for her mother, Rene Nash, a renowned teller of dialect stories. After Rene's death, Liz soon found that "the mantle had come to gently rest upon my shoulders". She appeared at the first Golowan *Tongue Pie* and has contributed ever since.

David Kemp is a sculptor who trained as a ship's officer. For the last 30 years he has lived amongst the ruined mines of West Penwith, recycling the discarded debris of consumer society as museum pieces of some uncertain future. He has made large site-specific sculptures throughout Britain, and more recently at the Eden Project. He is a landscape painter, and has collaborated with Kneehigh Theatre to produce outdoor theatre projects based on specific Cornish sites and issues. He has recently turned his hand to a bit of scribbling.

Jan Macfarlane was born and grew up on the banks of Loch Lomond, close to where her ancestors had, for generations, made their living from stealing cattle. She has lived in Cornwall for a quarter of a century, working as a doctor, raising some children, gardening, and writing a little.

Marie Macneill was educated at Penzance Girls Grammar School and trained as an actress at the Central School of Speech & Drama in London. She was artistic director of Bedside Manners and has written extensively for theatre and television. She currently has several commissioned feature films in development, a drama series for S4C and another for the BBC. She is artistic director of Mundic Nation and recently directed *Prime Fillet*, a film set in Penryn.

Bernard Moore was born in 1873 of Cornish parentage and spent much of his early life at St Germans. He walked the entire Cornish coast between 1897 and 1898. His published collections of verse include *Cornish Catches*, *A Cornish Haul*, *A Cornish Chorus*, *Cornish Corners*, *A Cornish Collection*, *A Cornish Gleaning* and *Cornish Crowsheaf*.

Annamaria Murphy writes for Scavel An Gow, Kneehigh, Alibi, Brainstorm Films, The Eden Project, and almost anyone who will have her. She most recently wrote for Kneehigh's *Tristan and Isuelt*, and is currently writing *The Visitation Of Roberto Collioni* for Platform 4. She lives in Paul with her daughter Georgia.

Jane Nancarrow was born at St Stephen's, Launceston, and was taught by Charles Causley at the old National V P School. She has been writing stories and poetry since her schooldays, but *The Perfect Cornish Christmas* is her first published work. She has just taken early retirement from teaching English after 30 years at Bodmin. She lives with her husband and family in Kirland but still considers herself "a Lanson maid" at heart.

Mick Paynter claims to have been born in Teetotal Street, St Ives, in 1948. Educated in St Ives, Penzance and Newcastle-on-Tyne, he works as a revenue officer in Penzance. A Bard of the Gorsedd, his published work includes *A Crowd Of Banners*.

David Penprase was born in Redruth in 1942. After a career in music with *Dave Lee and the Staggerlees*, he took up photography. A committed monochrome printer, and adjudicator for The Royal Photographic Society, he has received numerous awards for his work, which has appeared in magazines, books, and on record covers. His published collections include *Untitled*, *Beyond The Edge*, and *Passion, Pleasure & Pain*, along with the compilation titles *Erotique*, *Nudes* and *Nude*.

Marjery Ruhrmund (née Tresise) was born on Bodmin Moor in 1929. Educated at Penzance Girls Grammar School and Truro Grammar School, she trained as a nurse in Truro and worked in various nursing posts for many years. She is married to respected art critic Frank Ruhrmund and has two daughters. Though she does not regard herself as a poet, her verse has been published in a number of Quaker magazines.

Michael Sagar Fenton is a Penzance-born writer and columnist, whose day jobs have included record shop owner, actor, zoo-keeper, estate agent and dairy farmer. He acts as public relations officer for Penlee Lifeboat. His published work includes *Penlee: The Loss Of A Lifeboat* and *Rosebud And The Newlyn Clearances*.

Tim Saunders is a poet, linguist and journalist who was brought up at Delabole and St Tudy. His published work includes *Benyn Bennrudh*, *The High Tide*, *The Wheel*, *Looking At The Mermaid*, *In Arthur's Cave*, *The Reason Why*, *Gol Snak Vud/Bude Jazz Festival*, and *Nothing Broken*. He is currently working on a film script and on a novel. A Bard of the Gorsedd, he lives in Wales.

Pauline Sheppard is a playwright and performer, who has lived and worked in Cornwall since 1972. As a writer, her concerns are universal issues set in Cornwall. *Dogs* (1992) deals with the philosophy of freedom and crossing borders when a group of travellers are evicted from wasteland, and *Dressing Granite* (1997) concerns the survival of the individual. Most recently she adapted *The Ordinalia* for performances in St Just (2000-2002), and is working with the writers' collective Scavel an Gow. She has a screenplay in development with North West Vision.

Ann Trevenen Jenkin is a writer, poet, lecturer, Cornish-speaker and activist. A founder member of Mebyon Kernow, vice president of the Celtic Congress, and Bard of the Gorsedd for more than forty years, she was the first woman Grand Bard (1997-2000). She helped to organise the Keskerdh Kernow walk to London in 1997, and was one of 26 who walked all the way. Her published work includes two books on Leedstown, *Cornwall: The Hidden Land* (with R.G. Jenkin), *Gwel Kernow: A Cornish View*, and *The Prayerbook Rebellion*.

Michael Williams is a writer and Bard of the Gorsedd. A Cornishman, he founded Bossiney Books and was in publishing for 25 years. He and his wife Sonia live in a cottage near St Teath where he continues to write and operate as a publishing and writing consultant. A member of the Council of the Ghost Club Society, he has just completed *Supernatural Dartmoor*.